Cupboards & Doors

in a weekend

Deena Beverley

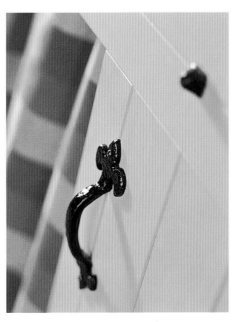

MEREHURST

For Clare and Ian – with gratitude for your friendship, and every
good wish for your future.

Acknowledgements

I would like to thank Anna Sanderson for once again giving me the opportunity
to explore new materials and acquire new skills. Thanks also to Anna for providing
many of the initial ideas from which the eventual projects developed. Many thanks to
Shelly, Dave and Graeme for working long and hard without complaint to produce the
step-by-step photography.

As always, I would also like to thank my husband and daughter for the patience and
support which they gave so unstintingly throughout that most demanding of times:
the period during which a wife and mother is engaged in completing a how-to book.

My husband, something of a master carpenter, endured and encouraged this, my
impatient initiation into constructional woodwork, with admirable tolerance. He
helped to make the previously uncharted waters of jigsawing, mitre cutting and
countersinking not only intelligible, but also enjoyable. I would like to say to every
reader that if I, with my limited enthusiasm for the less decorative aspects of DIY, can
master these processes then there is hope for us all.

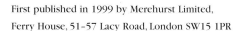

First published in 1999 by Merehurst Limited,
Ferry House, 51–57 Lacy Road, London SW15 1PR

Copyright © 1999 Merehurst Limited

ISBN 1 85391 799 0

A catalogue record for this book is available from the British Library.

Project Editor: Rowena Curtis
Design & Art Direction: Laura Jackson
Designer: Anita Ruddell
Photographer: Graeme Ainscough
Stylist: Caroline Davis
Template illustrations: King & King Associates
Commissioning Editor: Anna Sanderson
Publishing Manager: Fia Fornari
Production Manager: Lucy Byrne
CEO & Publisher: Anne Wilson
International Sales Director: Kevin Lagden
Marketing & Sales Director: Kathryn Harvey

Colour separation by Colourscan, Singapore
Printed in Singapore by Tien Wah Press

Contents

Introduction *6*

Floral fingerplate and doorknob set *8*

Citrus kitchen cupboard *12*

Utilizing a pantry door *18*

Seashore bathroom cabinet *24*

Stripping and finishing a pine door *30*

Romantic cupboard *34*

Transforming a plain, flush door *38*

Cottage-style door *44*

Country kitchen makeover *48*

Tool storage door *54*

Wardrobe with fabric-lined doors *58*

Adding privacy to a half-glazed door *62*

Child's fantasy wardrobe *68*

Glossary *74*

Suppliers *76*

Templates *77*

Index *80*

Introduction

Doors and cupboards are taken for granted, yet they are one of the most defining parts of a room's decor, and their decorative potential is often overlooked. Uninspired flush doors are often crying out for new life and soulless cupboard units are in dire need of personality. This book has been devised with real life problems firmly in mind: the kitchen cupboards that you cannot afford to replace but which torment you every time you think of them; the doors that are not important enough to warrant replacement, but which could benefit from a makeover.

The decorating methods used throughout provide a broad mixture of techniques, so that the projects can be adapted for whatever door or cupboard you need to update. For example, the tongue-and-groove technique has been successfully applied to both the country-style kitchen cupboard and the cottage door. All the projects are achievable with the most scant carpentry skills and some, such as the romantic cupboard and the deceptively complex looking painted panelled door, require no woodworking at all. As you progress, you will become more confident and will build on existing skills, becoming so proficient that you will soon be devising your own projects from scratch. Sometimes there is no need for power tools to give a new look. It may be an overstated decorating cliché to say that changing handles and other ironmongery gives an instant facelift to tired cupboards and doors, but the effects are so immediate and simply achieved that it is worth reiterating here.

Consider the mood of a piece before buying a new handle. The softened, layered colours of the painted panelled door require a suitably subtle, demi-matt handle, but the irrepressibly zingy palette of the child's fantasy wardrobe demands vivid, saturated colours in a contemporary, high gloss finish. Handles are available in a staggering array of designs. It is worth buying the best you can afford – adding a really special handle to a cupboard or door can elevate it from mass produced blandness to a slick design statement. Cheaper handles may have visible seams where they emerged from the mould, and never quite confer the luxury status they attempt to convey.

If you are on a limited budget, customize door and cupboard furniture yourself. The driftwood effect handle on the seashore cabinet is easily made from a piece of a dowel and a wooden 'pebble' from a packet of pot pourri. Similarly, the pretty three-dimensional roses on the romantic cupboard are cheap and easy to make, and have a handmade charm that could never be replicated by their smooth, china equivalent.

Practicality is a prime consideration when devising treatments for doors and cupboards, since both are in constant use. Water based paints have been used throughout, chosen for their ease of use, fast drying nature, simple clean-up, and low toxicity. Even unprotected, they prove resilient in everyday use, but their longevity will be dramatically improved with the addition of acrylic varnish. This has the same non-toxic, fast drying properties of emulsion and acrylic paints, and offers washability and added strength to painted surfaces. Apply as many layers as you can for optimum durability, allowing each coat to dry before applying the next.

All the projects in the book have been designed to be genuinely achievable within a weekend, and many of them will be completed far more quickly than this. The secret to success with all of them is planning. Not only will this make the project's completion more speedy but you will enjoy the whole experience much more if you have bought everything you need before starting work. Careful consideration of the piece which confronts you, or knowing the exact sizes you are looking for will save confusion in the shop. That said, it is the random nature of a project's completion that can prove to be the most pleasurable and satisfying part of 'doing-it-yourself'. Not only will you end up with something utterly unique, and maybe quite different to what you originally planned, but you will have had tremendous fun getting there too.

Deena Beverley

Floral finger plate and door knob set

This charming alternative to the pastel-toned finger plates available today updates the floral theme with its exuberantly scattered rosebuds and intense colouring.

If at first glance the hand-painted floral design on this project seems daunting look more closely. You will see that what initially appears a complex design is actually comprised of a simple layering technique, which is inspired by canal art. The flowers are built up using a technique known as 'blocking-in'. First, the rough shape of the flower or leaf is laid down using a pale tone. Subsequent layers of paint are then added using increasingly darker tones. By using just a few basic colours, then gradually lightening or darkening them with the addition of white or raw umber, you can be assured of colours that will appear natural and perfectly well matched.

The key to success with this project is to be as relaxed and spontaneous as possible when painting the floral motifs. There is no need to draw out accurate templates, and indeed complex pencil outlines would be very difficult to cover in paint. A simple circle for a flower-head, or an oval for a leaf, will suffice. The design is built up using swirling, curved strokes, rather like commas. Always follow the direction in which the actual flower or leaf grows and even the simplest stroke will look three-dimensional. Remember that you are aiming to capture the spirit of the flower, not attempting a botanically accurate rendition. Look at some floral fabrics to see examples of how effectively a rose can be portrayed using just a few colours and bold lines.

Day One

Step 1

On a 115 x 320mm (4½ x 12½in) rectangle of 6mm (¼in) thick MDF (medium-density fibreboard) mark four lines with a pencil, 25mm (1in) in from each edge. Drill a 25mm (1in) diameter hole at each intersection.

Step 2

Ensure that the MDF is well secured, then cut with a saw to the inside of each of the marked lines, making four cuts in total.

Step 3

Repeat steps 1 and 2 on a 105 x 310mm (4 x 12in) rectangle of 4mm (⅛in) thick MDF, then rub down both pieces to remove any flaws.

Step 4

Stick the smaller rectangle on top of the larger rectangle with wood glue and leave to set. Hold in place while the glue is drying with G-cramps.

Step 5

Rub down both the finger plate and the door knob until smooth. Wipe clean with a damp cloth to remove the sanding debris, then paint with cream emulsion paint. Leave both to dry thoroughly. Rub down again, very lightly, then wipe before painting with another coat of cream emulsion.

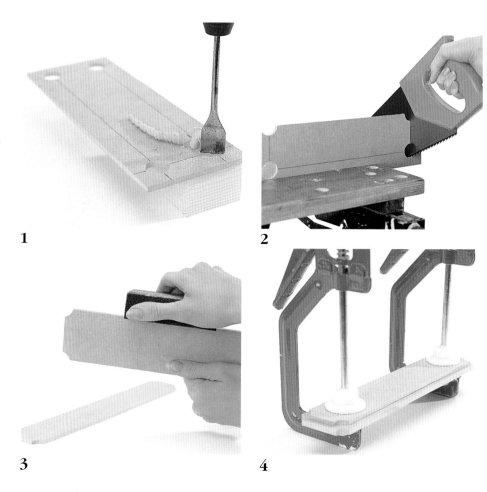

1

2

3

4

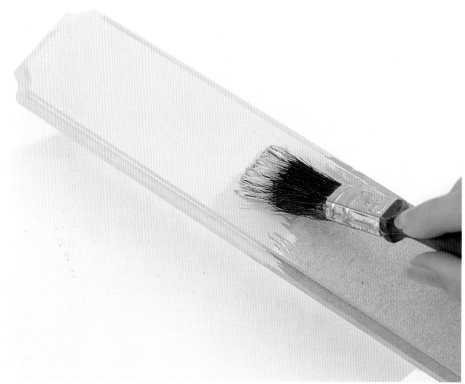

5

6

7

8

9

Day Two

Step 6
Transfer the rough position of the flowers and leaves on to the door knob and finger plate using a very soft pencil. If necessary, use the templates on page 77 as a guide to positioning the floral motifs.

Step 7
Put small amounts of the dark green, cream and dark crimson acrylic paints on a plate covered with tin foil. The plate will act as an easy-to-clean palette. Mix both the green and crimson paints with the cream to produce subtly graduated tones. Paint the design. Start by 'blocking in' the leaf and flower shapes with a pale tone, gradually adding darker tones on top using relaxed, broad, curved strokes which follow the natural direction in which a petal or leaf grows. Leave to dry.

Step 8
Varnish the door knob and finger plate, using an acrylic varnish. Apply several coats, allowing the varnish to dry thoroughly between coats.

Step 9
Attach the door knob and finger plate to the door with a grip fill adhesive, or alternatively use the fixing supplied with the door knob.

Flower power

Decorate a door knob and finger plate to complement the design of a room, perhaps using simple floral motifs copied from the curtains or other soft furnishings.

Citrus kitchen cupboard

This dressing up of existing melamine kitchen unit doors produces a sophisticated result far removed from the original, uninspiring finish.

Melamine is tough, easy to clean and inexpensive. As a result it has been universally popular with kitchen manufacturers for the past 50 years or so. The question most consistently asked of home interest magazines and television programmes is how to transform existing melamine units.

This project has been designed to ease the style nightmares of all those home owners unfortunate enough to have inherited a perfectly practical melamine kitchen in a truly unlovely colour. Avocado and hessian effect are still, sadly, with us. However, even a textured melamine surface will respond favourably to this elegant top dressing created with a combination of mitred mouldings, découpage and paint.

The key to the reassuringly solid look of the finished cupboard lies in scrupulous attention to filling. If the place where the mitred panel meets the door is left unfilled it will be revealed as a dark line, giving away the fact that this is an applied treatment. However, if the join is filled the door will appear to have been constructed from solid wood, giving an authentic, heavy looking finish far removed from the original thin melamine.

Choose découpage motifs to suit the decorative theme of your kitchen. The lemons and leaves motifs used in this project were cut from the generous samples that are available from wallpaper retailers, although you may need to invest in a whole roll if you are updating your entire kitchen.

Planning your time

DAY ONE
AM: Remove and prepare doors. Measure for mitred frame and cut lengths of moulding
PM: Glue and panel pin mitred frame on to door. Pin to secure. Fill

DAY TWO
AM: Prepare door with liquid sander. Paint door and handle. Stencil on script. Apply découpage motifs

PM: Varnish door. Affix handle

Tools and materials

Screwdriver

Sanding block and sandpaper

Knotting fluid and cotton bud

Tape measure

Pencil

Simple moulding

Handsaw

Mitre saw

Wood adhesive

Panel pins

Hammer

Nail punch

Filler and filler knife

Liquid sander and cloth

Paintbrush and paint kettle

Grey and cream emulsion paints; yellow, grey, raw umber and white acrylic paints

Plate and tin foil

Natural sponge

Stencil and stencil brushes

Repositionable spray adhesive

Wallpaper or gift wrap

PVA adhesive and brush

Varnish and brush

New handle

Day One

Step 1
Remove the cupboard door and rub down to remove debris. Wipe with a damp cloth to remove sanding dust.

Step 2
Apply knotting fluid to any knots on the mouldings with a cotton bud. Leave the fluid to set according to the manufacturer's instructions.

Step 3
Measure along the outside edge of the face of the door. Cut a length of moulding slightly longer than this measurement, which will make accurate cutting much easier. Set the mitre saw to 45 degrees, towards the left. Place the moulding on the saw, flat face against the back plate of the saw, curved face towards you. Hold the moulding securely in place as you make the first cut, keeping the blade upright.

Step 4
Measure from this cut along the longer flat edge to the same length as the outside edge of the cupboard face. Set the mitre saw to 45 degrees, this time to the right. Place the piece of moulding in the saw again, flat side to the back plate as before, then make the second cut.

Step 5
Repeat steps 3 and 4 to produce the remaining three lengths of mitred moulding which will form the frame which sits on the door surface. Check each opposing pair for length. Sand to adjust length if necessary. This is much easier than trying to cut off a tiny sliver of wood with the mitre saw.

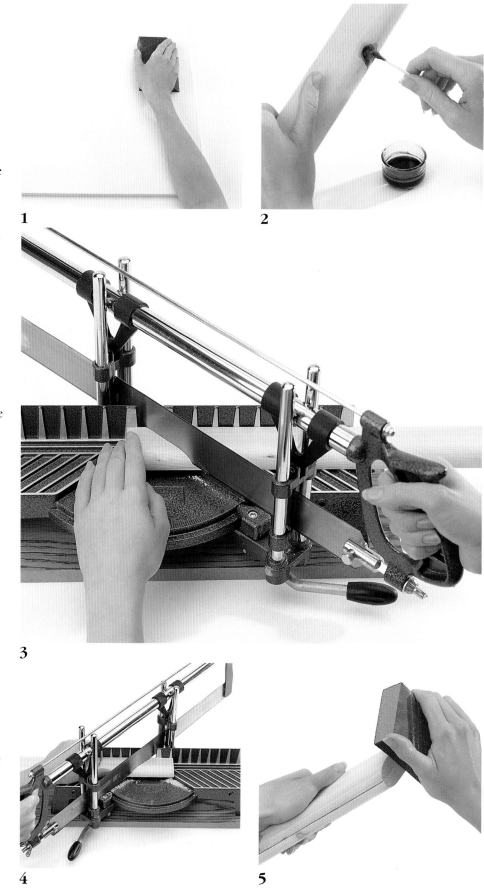

1

2

3

4

5

6

7

8

Step 6

After a trial fitting of the frame to the door front, apply wood adhesive to the mouldings and glue them firmly on to the front of the door.

Step 7

To secure the frame, hammer panel pins in through the mouldings and into the door at regular intervals.

Step 8

Tap the panel pins just below the surface of the wood, using a nail punch, in order to achieve a smooth finish.

Step 9

Using a fine surface filler, fill any gaps in the mitred joints or where the frame sits on the door and any other general inadequacies in the surface of the wood, for example where pins or knots appear. Leave the door to dry.

Mitre magic

At first glance, mitre saws look much more complex than they actually are to use. Mastery of the mitre saw is quick to acquire and will ease the transformation of many flat surfaces.

9

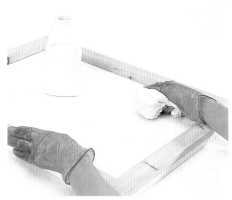

10

Day Two

Step 10

Prepare the door and the applied moulding with a liquid sander, following the manufacturer's directions. This will provide a good key for the paint, ensuring uniform and lasting paint adhesion.

Step 11

Paint the entire door, including the moulding frame, with emulsion paint, sponging on and dry brushing layers of colour to achieve a soft, diffused finish. A plate covered with tin foil makes a good palette, which does not need to be cleaned as the tin foil can be thrown away after use.

Step 12

Lightly spray the reverse of a script stencil with a repositionable spray adhesive. Place this on the door, and stencil on the script using soft tones mixed from the acrylic paints. Mix the paints as you work to achieve a random look – the script will need to be pale, almost white, as it passes over the grey of the frame, but darker as it passes over the yellow sponging of the door.

11

12

13

14

15

Step 13

Cut out and apply the découpage motifs to the door using PVA adhesive. When the glue is dry lightly sponge another layer of paint over the découpage motifs to blend them into the door design.

Step 14

When the paint is fully dry, varnish the whole door using several coats of varnish, allowing each coat to dry thoroughly before adding the next.

Step 15

Re-hang the cupboard door. Finally, fix the new handle in place.

Matching handles

The handle purchased for this project looked too new so it was prepared with a liquid sander and painted lightly with subdued tones of acrylic paint, then varnished, to match the door more closely.

Utilizing a pantry door

Additional food storage space is always welcome. These simple but effective solutions maximise the overlooked space on the back of a pantry door.

There is never enough space in a larder, particularly for the diverse range of containers that inhabit the kitchen of the keen cook. If items are not easy to see and reach they may be forgotten until their sell-by date has passed. As well as utilizing an otherwise redundant space, this project improves the storage solutions afforded by a cupboard or pantry as a whole, by making particularly small, difficult-to-store items immediately accessible and providing a home for tall bottles that normally shield small items from view, while occupying valuable shelf space.

The mixture of materials used here is unified by painting them to match the door. Emulsion paint is quick and clean to work with, and is protected with acrylic varnish. Eggshell paint would be a suitable alternative, as it is durable, with an appealing soft sheen, but it does take longer to dry. Water based eggshell paint is now available and does not have the problem of noxious smells and messy, spirit based brush cleaning associated with normal eggshell paint. This product does not need varnishing.

The shelves and rack are fixed to the door with cavity fixings specifically designed for cavity or flush doors. The word 'cavity' is actually a slight misnomer – although only the sides, top and bottom are made of solid wood (for the secure fixing of hinges, handles and locks), the core is generally a strong sandwich of compressed board. The cavity fixings, which spring open within the door to provide a strong gripping anchor, combined with the design of these shelves (which places the load so that each shelf is pushed in towards the door, not hanging away from it) make this project a strong and reliable way to add storage space to any cavity or flush door.

Planning your time

DAY ONE
AM: Make shelves and paint

PM: Make spice rack and paint

PM: Paint second coat. Spray paint chicken wire

DAY TWO
AM: Sand door, fix shelves. Paint

PM: Varnish

Tools and materials

Piece of 12mm (½in) thick plywood

Templates (pages 78–9)

Jigsaw

Pencil

Tape measure

Straight edge

Drill

1.5mm (¹⁄₂₀in), 3mm (¹⁄₁₆in), 4mm (⅛in) and 6mm (¼in) drill bits

Bradawl

Countersink

1¼in No.8 countersunk wood screws

Filler and filling knife

Sandpaper and sanding block

Damp cloth

Handsaw

Panel saw

8.5mm (⅓in) diameter dowel

Wood glue

Coloured insulating tape

Liquid sander (optional)

Emulsion paint

Flush door cavity fixings

Paintbrush and paint kettle

Acrylic varnish and varnish brush

1

Day One

Step 1

Prepare to make the two shelves. Using a jigsaw, and following the templates on pages 78-9, cut pieces A, B, C, D, E, F and G from a piece of 12mm (½in) thick plywood. Cut two each of pieces A, B, C and G as these form the back, sides and base of both shelves.

Step 2

Drill and countersink 4mm (⅛in) holes in each piece of plywood, as indicated on the templates.

Step 3

Loosely assemble the cut pieces of plywood to form the two shelves. Mark pilot holes with a bradawl.

2

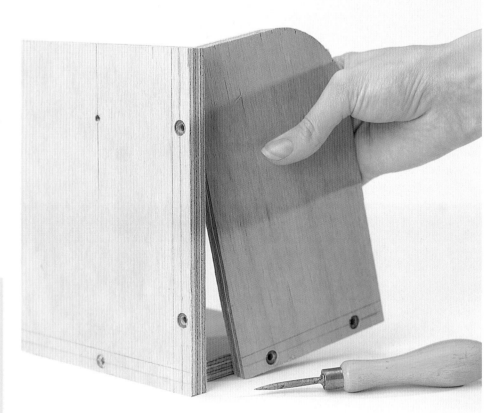

3

Saving space

These simple and easy-to-make storage shelves are extremely adaptable, making them a useful, space-saving addition to any bedroom, bathroom or box room.

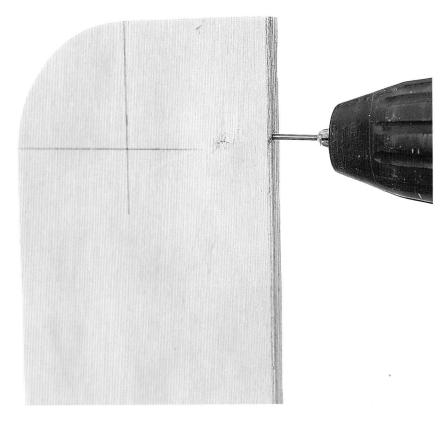

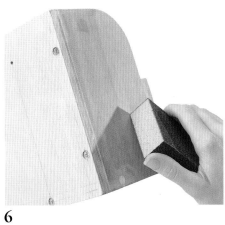

6

Step 4
Drill the pilot holes in each of the
pieces of plywood, using the 1.5mm
($\frac{1}{20}$in) drill bit.

Step 5
Assemble the pieces of plywood to
make the two shelves, using 1¼in No.8
countersunk wood screws.

Step 6
Fill the screw holes and joins with a
quick-setting fine surface filler. Sand
both shelves lightly with the sanding
block in preparation for painting, then
wipe with a damp cloth to remove
sanding debris. There is no need to fill
the holes on the back of the two
shelves, the surfaces of which will
be against the door.

4

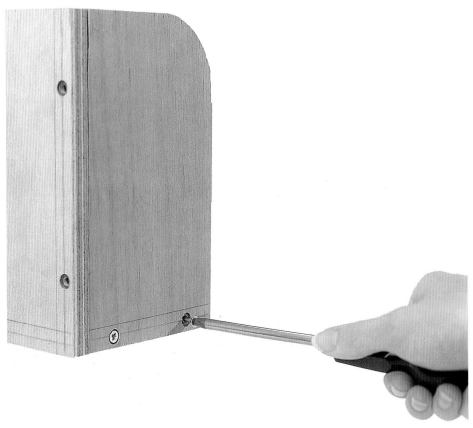

5

Step 7

Using a handsaw, cut the baseboard for the spice rack from a piece of 12mm (½in) thick plywood, following the template on page 79.

Step 8

Cut a length of 8.5mm (⅓in) diameter dowel into 56mm (2¼in) lengths with a panel saw.

Step 9

Mark out dowel locating holes with a pencil on the baseboard of the spice rack. Mark the holes to suit the width of your spice jars. Drill 6mm (¼in) deep into the baseboard. Prop up one long side of the piece of wood you are drilling into on an offcut of the 12mm (½in) thick plywood. This means that the holes will be placed at a perfect angle so that the lengths of dowel will be slightly slanted, making the spice jars sit more securely on the rack. Drill fixing holes at each end of the rack.

Step 10

Glue the lengths of dowel in place on the spice rack with wood glue.

Step 11

Remove any excess glue whilst it is still wet. Sand the whole rack lightly, then wipe away the sanding dust in preparation for painting.

Judging drill depths

Wrap a length of coloured insulating tape around a drill bit at the required depth. When the tape touches the surface of the piece of wood you are drilling into you will know you have drilled deep enough.

7

8

9

10

11

12

13

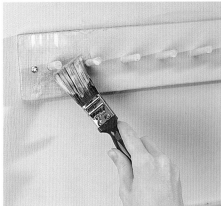

14

Day Two

Step 12

Lightly sand the surface of the door with fine sandpaper to provide a key. Wipe with a damp cloth to remove the sanding dust. Alternatively, apply liquid sander, following the manufacturer's directions. Paint the door with one coat of emulsion paint, then leave to dry.

Step 13

Fix the shelves and the spice rack to the door, using lengths of flush door cavity fixings that are appropriate to the thickness of the door and following the manufacturer's directions.

Step 14

Paint the shelves and the spice rack with emulsion paint, adding more layers if necessary for good opaque coverage. Allow each coat to dry thoroughly before applying the next. When completely dry, varnish with acrylic matt varnish.

Seashore bathroom cabinet

This junk shop bargain was originally covered with self-adhesive vinyl. It certainly deserved a new and more stylish look.

The shape and size of this cupboard had great potential. Never be put off by an unattractive finish on existing cupboards and doors. As long as the woodwork underneath is sound, the piece can be quickly and easily brought up to date. Modern surface preparations, referred to generically as liquid sanders, make painting all sorts of hitherto unpaintable surfaces a breeze. This means that where once you would have had to carefully strip the gloss paint off an old door before repainting it, or laboriously sand it to a uniformly matt finish, now you simply apply a proprietary product and then paint directly over the old paint.

This seashore-inspired design uses a crackle medium, applied between two layers of emulsion paint, to create an aged look reminiscent of weather-worn beach huts. The old style two-part crackle glazes were difficult to apply successfully, but technological advances in paint finishes mean that this type of effect is easy to reproduce with no previous experience in paint effects at all.

The frame which holds the seashore finds was inexpensively made by a picture framer to the required size and depth to fit the cupboard used in this project, although you may strike lucky and find a frame of precisely the right dimensions in your local chain store. This type of frame, often known as a 'shadowbox', has a certain depth between the glass and the backing board of the frame, which makes it ideal for displaying three-dimensional designs.

Planning your time

DAY ONE

AM: Prepare cupboard. Cut hole in door for frame. Glue frame front in place. Stick paper to backing board

PM: Paint cupboard, backing board and frame. Apply crackle medium and add top coat of paint

DAY TWO

AM: Arrange and glue items in place on backing board

PM: Add small items to frame; fix backing board in place. Make and affix handle

Tools and materials

Screwdriver

Sanding block and sandpaper

Set square

Pencil

Metal ruler

Drill and 8mm (⅜ in) drill bit

Jigsaw and blade

Glue gun and glue sticks

'Shadowbox' type picture frame

Wallpaper or gift wrap

Spray glue

Craft knife and blades

Masking tape

Dark aqua and aqua emulsion paint

Crackle glaze

Paintbrush

Leaf skeletons, feathers and seaweed

Shells and sand

Glass shell shapes and nuggets

Seashore-type pot pourri mix

Adhesive tape

Wooden 'pebble'

Piece of dowel

Wood adhesive

Raffia

Day One

Step 1

Remove the old handle from the cupboard. Rub down the whole cupboard to clear any surface debris. Wipe the cupboard over with a damp cloth to remove sanding dust.

Step 2

Measure the 'shadowbox' frame, then draw out the area with a ruler and pencil on the cupboard front where the frame is to be placed. The hole should be slightly smaller than the frame so that it holds the frame in place.

Step 3

Drill a hole, using an 8mm (⅜in) drill bit, just inside each corner of this marked area on the cupboard front.

Step 4

Insert the jigsaw blade through one of the drilled holes and cut out the marked area.

Step 5

Sand the edges of the hole smooth with a sanding block, then wipe away the sanding dust with a damp cloth.

1

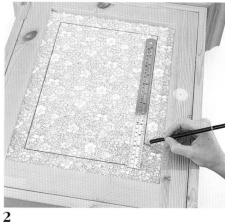

2

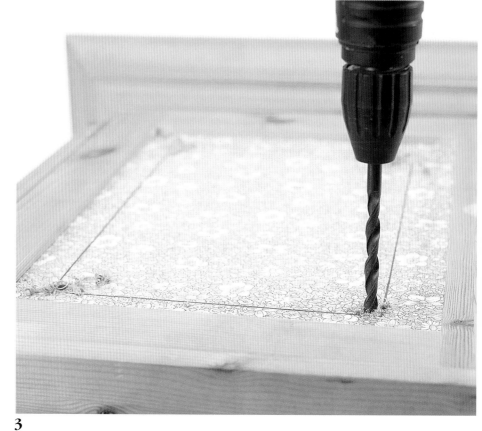

3

4

5

7

Step 6
Place the frame carefully into the hole in the cupboard door that was cut to size in steps 2–5. Secure the frame in position at the rear of the door using a glue gun.

Step 7
Attach an oversized piece of wallpaper or gift wrap (chosen to co-ordinate with your design) to the side of the frame backing board which will face the glass, using spray glue. Using a craft knife, trim the paper down to the exact size of the board.

Step 8
Mask off the glass of the frame with tape. Paint the dark aqua base coat on the cupboard, inside the frame and on the back of the frame board, painting in the direction of the grain. Leave to dry.

Step 9
Paint the crackle glaze on all the external faces of the cupboard, following the manufacturer's directions.

Step 10
Paint the cupboard with a top coat of aqua paint. The type of crackle glaze used for this project requires that the top coat of paint is applied at right angles to the first coat, in this case against the grain.

10

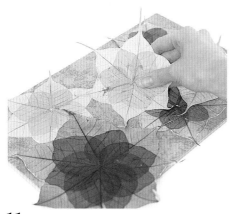

11

Day Two

Step 11
Arrange the leaf skeletons or any other flat parts of the design, such as pressed leaves or seaweed, loosely on the covered backing board of the frame. Use adhesive spray to fix in position.

Step 12
Glue gun all the other items that make up the design, such as feathers, shells, glass nuggets and driftwood, in place on the backing board.

Step 13
Place a small amount of sand, shells and other seashore finds loosely in the picture frame itself, before replacing the back on the frame. Using the glue gun and adhesive tape, secure the back panel of the frame in place.

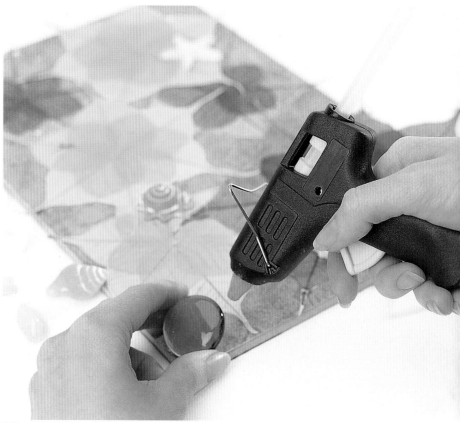

12

13

16

14

Step 14
Paint the tape holding the frame in position with the same dark aqua base paint as the rest of the interior of the cupboard.

Step 15
Make a handle by cutting a short length of dowel, then drilling a small recess in a wooden 'pebble' and a corresponding recess in the door. Glue the 'pebble' on to the dowel with wood adhesive.

Step 16
Glue the handle on to the door and, finally, tie a piece of raffia around the 'pebble' for a decorative touch.

Themed displays

The basic design of this cupboard could be adapted to suit any room in the house. For example, painted in sombre browns and greens and filled with masculine ephemera such as fishing flies or even old school mementoes, it would look great in any study or living room.

15

Stripping and finishing a pine door

Removing layers of gloss paint to uncover a pure wooden door is truly satisfying, and the finished door will enhance a room dramatically.

If you have many doors to strip, then it is recommended that this task be tackled by a company specializing in wood stripping. These companies will strip the doors using chemical methods on a scale that is simply not practical in a domestic setting. Your doors will be ready more quickly than you could hope to achieve when working at home and, usually, at quite a reasonable price.

That said, it is immensely pleasing to gradually remove an applied surface and reveal the naked wood beneath and it is certainly viable to strip doors at home. Removing paint can become positively therapeutic, as the layers drop away beneath the touch of blow torch, wire brush or chemical stripper. Realistically, most surfaces usually require a mixture of all the paint removal techniques, depending on the complexity of mouldings and the composition and thickness of the paint layers.

Having uncovered the wood there are many decorative options from which to choose. If the bare wood is simply varnished, it usually turns an unwelcome shade of shiny yellow, and not the discreet tone envisaged. Using a coloured wax in a subtle shade such as 'antique pine', or 'oak' gives a soft, classical look that fits in equally well with contemporary or modern decor. Alternatively, transparent, coloured wood dyes are available in a wide range of colours, from rose pink to fluorescent purple. They work particularly well in children's rooms, where vivid colour is generally welcomed.

Coloured varnish is a really quick way to achieve the sort of wood finish that was so beloved by the Victorians in the 19th century: rich in colour with a visible grain and a deep, glossy sheen. A more contemporary Swedish look, redolent of scrubbed, greyish floorboards, is simply achieved with some clever paint trickery, fast forwarding a new door into antiqued shabby chic splendour.

Planning your time

DAY ONE
AM: Prepare work area. Apply stripper. Scrape off old paint

PM: Continue stripping. Rinse surface well and dispose of waste

DAY TWO
AM: Sand, wipe with damp rag

PM: Apply chosen finish. Replace handle

Tools and materials

Screwdriver(s)

Disposable bin liners

Dust sheets and old newspapers

Protective overalls/gloves/goggles

Paint stripper and old paintbrush

Shave hook/scraper

Sanding block and sandpaper

Electric sander (optional)

Damp cloth

Disposable rags

Replacement door handle (optional)

Wax finish:
'Antique pine' coloured wax

Wire wool

Soft cloth or buffing brush

Coloured finish:
Coloured dye and brush

Matt varnish and brush

Victorian finish:
Coloured varnish and brush

Appropriate clear varnish (see manufacturer's instructions)

Swedish style finish:
Raw umber and black acrylic paints

White emulsion or acrylic paint

Paintbrush

Plate and tin foil

Kitchen paper

Matt varnish and brush

Wax finish

Coloured finish

Victorian finish

Swedish style finish

Day One

Step 1

Remove the door handle and other door furniture, such as coat hooks and finger plates. Prepare the area by placing a bin with a disposable liner within reach, spreading dust sheets and/or old newspaper sheets all around and by putting on protective overalls, gloves and goggles. Paint on the chemical paint/varnish stripper and leave for approximately 10–30 minutes, as recommended by the manufacturer.

Step 2

Using a flat scraper, scrape off the congealed paint and stripper from the large, flat areas of the door on to pieces of old newspaper. Place these carefully in the bin.

Step 3

Continue to remove the stripped paint, using a shave hook to scrape away the debris from the fiddly smaller areas, such as the mouldings. Strip the door handle if you wish to use it again. Using disposable rags, thoroughly rinse off any remaining stripper with water. If a substantial amount of paint is still stubbornly present, you may need to repeat steps 1–3 at this point in order to remove it.

Day Two

Step 4

When the door has been completely stripped and dried, sand thoroughly. An electric sander makes light work of this task. Finish with fine sand paper or sanding block, then wipe off the residual dust with a damp cloth.

1

2

3

Using paint stripper

Switch on the answer phone and eat and drink before starting work as it is both messy and dangerous to juggle caustic paint stripper with these basic requirements. Collect paint stripper and old paint as you work and place in the bin to avoid mess; tie the bin bag and dispose of when finished.

4

Wax finish

Step 1
Rub on a small amount of wax with fine grade wire wool. We used an 'antique pine' wax. Use a circular motion to apply and finish each application in line with the grain of the wood. Continue until the whole door has been waxed. Wax the handle as well if using a wooden handle.

Step 2
When the wax is dry, usually after about 30 minutes to 1 hour, buff the door with a soft cotton cloth or soft brush until a gentle sheen is achieved. Leaving some wax to harden in the corners of the mouldings gives an authentic, aged appearance. Finally, replace the door handle.

Coloured finish

Step 1
Brush the coloured dye on to the door with a paintbrush. Start by working across the grain, ensuring that the dye fills every pore of the wood. Finish by brushing in the direction of the grain. Appy sufficient dye to cover the door evenly, but not so much that it runs down the door.

Step 2
When the coloured dye is completely dry, brush the door with a coat of matt varnish. To increase the resilience of this finish, add several further coats of matt varnish. Allow each coat to dry thoroughly before applying the next. Always wash out all varnish brushes after use.

Victorian finish

Step 1
Brush on the varnish, working across the grain initially to ensure that it fills every pore of the wood. Finish by brushing in the direction of the grain. Allow the varnish to dry thoroughly before applying additional coats if required (for added durability and greater depth of colour).

Step 2
To add durability to the finish without affecting the colour, simply add a coat of the clear varnish recommended by the manufacturers for optimum compatibility with the coloured varnish. Clean the brush thoroughly in the recommended solvent and allow to dry before applying this final coat.

Swedish style finish

Step 1
Working on a plate covered with tin foil, rub dashes of raw umber and black acrylic paint randomly on to the door with a cloth. Leave to dry for about 30 minutes. Do not be alarmed if the door looks rather odd at this stage; many paint effects look unconvincingly unattactive until complete.

Step 2
Make a 50:50 mixture of white paint and water. Stir and brush on the door in the direction of the grain. Work quickly so as not to leave noticeable brush strokes. Rub the paint with kitchen paper to soften the effect; again working in the direction of the grain. When the door is dry apply a coat of matt varnish.

Romantic cupboard

This charming fabric-covered cupboard had long since lost its mirrored front, rendering it quite useless. Mounting board fills the gap without the need for complex carpentry.

This project grew from a desire to create a highly decorative finish simply by applying various treatments to an existing piece, without needing to purchase and fit replacement handles, hinges, mirror glass and other items.

The fragile-looking rose door and drawer knobs are quite deceptive. They are actually amazingly strong as they are constructed from quite an unlikely material: the same two-part putty that is used to repair broken plumbing. This epoxy putty is widely available from DIY shops and, surprisingly perhaps, china and toy shops, since it has a multiplicity of uses from fixing teapots to making porcelain-like dolls.

The putty is deeply therapeutic to work with. Use it with water to create a pliable, uniform consistency that can be filed and sanded to an even greater smoothness when dry. Although the roses look quite sophisticated in their construction they take literally moments to make. Detailed instructions for use are supplied with the sets of rose petal cutters that are available from cake decorating suppliers; most of which come in a variety of sizes to suit the dimensions of the knobs that you are covering.

Planning your time

DAY ONE
AM: Sand and paint cupboard. Cover drawers and door panel with fabric

PM: Cover parts of cupboard with wallpaper. Make roses

DAY TWO
AM: Paint and varnish roses

PM: Glue panel in place. When dry, remove masking tape

Tools and materials

Sanding block and sandpaper
Power sander and sanding sheets
Blue paint
Paintbrush
Fabric
Scissors
Multipurpose spray adhesive
Scalpel and blades
Mounting board
Tape measure
Pencil
Metal ruler
Set square
Wallpaper sample
Tracing paper
Cutting mat
Craft knife and blades
Masking tape
Set of cake decorators' rose petal cutters
Smooth chopping board
Rolling pin
Epoxy putty/modelling medium
Plate and tin foil
Acrylic paint in mid and dark pink
Artists' paintbrushes, sizes 3 and 5
Varnish and brush

Day One

Step 1

Rub down the cupboard, door and drawers. Wipe over with a damp cloth to remove dust. You may need to power sand the drawers to leave sufficient room for the fabric, while still allowing the smooth movement of the drawers.

1

2

Step 2

Paint the cupboard inside and out to tone with the fabric.

Step 3

Drape a piece of fabric over one of the drawers, any prominent motif centrally placed. Snip to allow the fabric to pass over the knob. Remove the fabric and spray the drawer front and reverse of the fabric with adhesive. Place the fabric on the drawer front again, smoothing it out neatly. Fold in and cut away excess fabric to form neat, mitred turns. Trim away excess fabric from around the knobs with a scalpel.

3

Step 4

Cut a piece of mounting board to fit behind the door frame. Roughly position an oversized piece of fabric on top of the mounting board to ascertain good positioning of motifs. Glue first one half, then the other half of the fabric on to the card to retain this position accurately. Fold over and neatly mitre fabric at the corners as for the drawers. To neaten the reverse of the panel and to decorate the interior, glue on a piece of wallpaper sample.

Step 5

Press tracing paper into any complex shapes on the cupboard to create templates for decorative insets of wallpaper. Cut the wallpaper to size and stick in place, starting from the centre to aid accurate placement. Trim with a scalpel for a perfect fit.

4

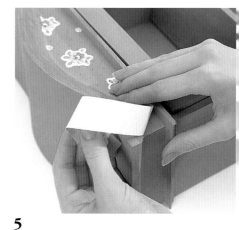

5

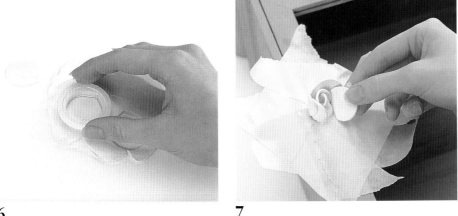

6 **7**

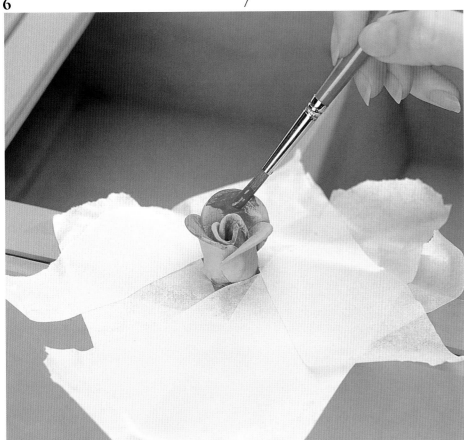

8

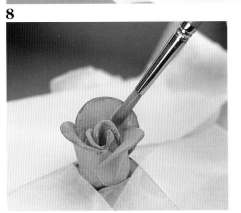

9

10

Step 6

Rub down the knobs, then mask off the surrounding area with masking tape. Follow the manufacturer's directions for the modelling medium; in this case, cut two identically sized pieces from the two parts supplied, knead well until colours are mixed, then knead for a further minute. Keeping your hands, rolling pin, and board wet for easy handling, roll out the clay to about 1mm (¹⁄₁₆ in) thick. Cut four petal shapes using the small rose petal cutter.

Step 7

Drape one petal shape over the knob and mould to fit tightly around knob, using a dampened finger. Apply the remaining three petals to the knob so that each subsequent petal is slightly tucked into the preceding petal. Tweak into shape and smooth with a wet finger. Repeat with three more petals, cut using a larger size of petal cutter. Leave to dry for 2–3 hours.

Day Two

Step 8

When the roses are completely dry, paint with mid-pink acrylic paint and leave to dry. Use tin foil over a plate as a convenient palette – the foil can simply be thrown away after use. Add a darker, carmine pink to give the roses more definition. Leave to dry.

Step 9

Varnish the roses and leave them to dry. Remove the masking tape from around the knobs.

Step 10

Glue the central, fabric-covered panel in place and secure with masking tape until the glue has set. Finally, remove the masking tape from the back of the door panel.

Transforming a plain, flush door

Flush doors are cheap, and easy to clean, yet not always lovely to look at. This moodily romantic panelled door started life in quite a different guise.

Calligraphy, and letter forms in all variations, have long held a powerful visual appeal for designers and home owners, particularly when their beauty is unhampered by immediate association with particular words. Hence the choice of Latin, as a largely unfamiliar language, for this project.

The elegance of the various letter shapes themselves speaks volumes; equally you could copy out a few lines from a favourite poem, or even a quotation, to personalize a door. The lyrics of a lullaby, for example, would look adorable on a nursery door, accompanied by similarly soothing motifs of twinkling stars and drifting clouds.

The mouldings which produce the panelled effect are ridiculously simple to apply. Available ready made, in inexpensive packs from DIY stores, they even have self-adhesive backing and a template for placing the mouldings accurately on the door. If you prefer to make your own mitred panels, see the Citrus kitchen cupboard project on pages 12–17, which gives advice on mitre cutting.

Even when painted a single, solid colour, with no further embellishment whatsoever, these panels will turn the most despicable fake wooden door into a neo-classical beauty. Liquid sander, another modern DIY superstar, aids the transformation by allowing uniform adhesion of paint to a shiny surface, and making the finish smooth and long lasting.

Planning Your Time

DAY ONE
AM: Remove door handle and prepare door. Mark position of panels. Apply panels

PM: Apply liquid sander. Paint layers of base colour on to door and architrave

DAY TWO
AM: Project, mark out, and paint text and flower motifs on to door

PM: Rub down motifs. Varnish door and architrave. Affix new handle

Tools and materials

Screwdriver

Sanding block and sandpaper

Damp cloth

Panel kit

Set square

Pencil

Liquid sander and cloth

Cream emulsion paint

Paintbrush

Paint kettle

Kitchen paper

Raw umber universal stainer

Greyish-blue emulsion paint

Greeny-blue emulsion paint

Broad emulsion brush

Projector

Text template photocopied on to acetate

White, black, crimson and green acrylic paints

Artists' brushes

Plate and tin foil

Floral motif template photocopied on to acetate

Acrylic varnish and brush

New handle and fixings

1

Day One

Step 1
Remove the old door handle and prepare the door by rubbing down with the sanding block to remove surface dirt and debris. Wipe over with a damp cloth to remove sanding dust.

Step 2
Using the template provided in the pack, mark out in pencil on the door where to place the self-adhesive panels. Attach the panels to the door following the manufacturer's instructions.

Step 3
Apply a liquid sander to both the door and the mouldings with a cloth, following the manufacturer's directions.

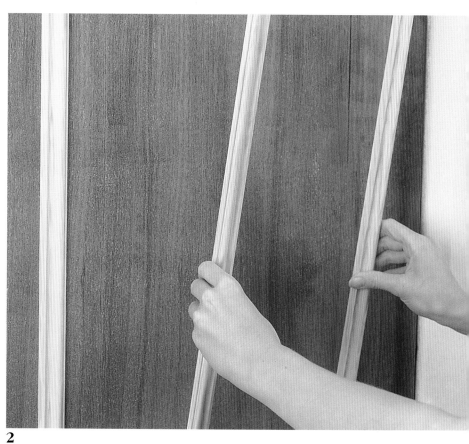

2

3

4

5

Step 4

Paint cream emulsion paint over the entire door and the architrave, then leave to dry.

Step 5

Mix a tiny amount of the raw umber stainer into the greyish-blue emulsion for an age-softened tone. Apply to the door and architrave using a dry brush, allowing a small amount of the base coat to show through. Leave to dry.

Step 6

Dilute the greeny-blue emulsion 50:50 with water, and apply carefully with a broad emulsion brush over the door and architrave, taking care not to disturb the paint beneath. Leave to dry.

Step 7

Paint on a final coat of cream paint, applying sparingly using a dry brush. Leave to dry thoroughly.

6

7

Brush works

Take care to apply the diluted emulsion paint to the door in the direction that the wood grain would lie on an old pine door, in order to create an authentic effect.

8

Day Two

Step 8
Prepare the text and set it up on the projector. Adjust the focus while projecting the text at the door until you are happy with the scale.

Step 9
Mix the black and white acrylic paints, using a plate covered in tin foil as a convenient, easy-to-clean palette. Fill in the text on the door with the pale grey acrylic paint, using light strokes.

Step 10
Project the flower motifs at the door, again adjusting the focus until you are happy with the scale. Pencil the motifs in place on the door.

Scissor happy
If the idea of painting text freehand terrifies you then use découpage letters instead. Photocopy text to enlarge it before cutting out the letters and adhering to the door. Seal with a coat of matt acrylic varnish.

9

10

11

12

Step 11
Paint the flowers and leaves on to the door with loose, painterly strokes. Use the crimson and green acrylic paints, making the paint dilute for a transparent finish. Allow to dry.

Step 12
Soften the word and flower motifs further with a sanding block. Remove sanding dust with a damp cloth.

Step 13
Apply several coats of acrylic varnish to the door and the architrave; allowing each coat to dry thoroughly before applying the next.

Step 14
Fix the new handle to the door. Use the fixings supplied by the manufacturer.

13

14

Projecting text

To produce film, scan or photocopy the text on to acetate, take a photograph of the page on slide (transparency) film or write on the acetate with a fine OHP pen.

Cottage-style door

Flush doors are inexpensive and easy to paint, but are lacking in the rustic charm department. This simple applied treatment gives an instant country appeal to an existing flat door.

Tongue-and-groove boards are applied to a flush door for a really convincing, solid looking country door with none of the problems encountered when trying to find a reclaimed door to fit a particular doorway. Invariably, the unique styles which make these old doors so visually appealing have their own inherent problems, such as random sizing, woodworm, warping or buckling.

Choosing appropriate door furniture is critical to producing an authentic result. It is not advisable to re-hang the door using strap hinges. Since the finished door carries the added weight of the boarding, it is best to hang it using the original hinges in the solid side panel of the flush door, reserving a pair of slightly adapted strap hinges as a decorative device only. The fixing plate of the hinge is simply hacksawed away, leaving a strap and rotating part which looks realistically operational.

The colour and texture of the paint chosen for this project is important. Stick to softer tones for a gentle finish and keep any varnish matt or slightly 'satinised' for a soothing look, that will blend well with surrounding decor.

Since this project revamps an existing door it is suitable for applications where the door cannot be replaced, for example in a rented home. Although it would be irritating to remove the tongue-and-groove once applied, it is possible. However, the finished country style result is so charming that it is unlikely that any landlord would choose to have the flush surface reinstated.

Planning your time

DAY ONE
AM: Remove door, sand lightly

PM: Cut tongue-and-groove.
Glue in position

DAY TWO
AM: Fill and apply knotting.
Sand door smooth. Paint

PM: Varnish. Add door furniture

Tools and materials

Screwdriver(s)

Sanding block and sandpaper

Pencil

Card

Handsaw

6 x 25mm (1in) thick
tongue-and-groove boards

Set square

Tape measure

Plane

Trestles (see page 46)

G-cramps

Adhesive

Panel pins

Hammer

Nail punch

Filler and filling knife

Clear knotting fluid

Old brush or rag

Damp cloth

Blue emulsion paint

Paintbrush and paint kettle

Varnish and varnish brush

Strap hinges

Thumb latch handle

Hacksaw and blades

Day One

Step 1

Remove the door from its hinges and take off the handle and any other door furniture, such as the coat hook or finger plate. Sand the face of the door lightly to provide a key for the glue.

Step 2

Measure, then cut the tongue-and-groove boards to the same length as the door, using a handsaw.

Step 3

Lay the door across two trestles and loosely position the tongue-and-groove boards centrally along the length of the door. Making sure that the boards do not slip, mark the underside of the two boards that fall at the long edges of the door with a pencil line. Use G-cramps, or speed cramps, to hold the boards securely in place whilst you do this.

Step 4

Trim the two edge boards with a saw, as marked, and sand smooth.

Step 5

Apply adhesive to the rear of one edge board. Position on the door and secure in place with panel pins that are long enough to penetrate the door by approximately 12mm (⅝in). Continuing to apply adhesive, position the tongue-and-groove boards across the width of the door until they are all are glued and panel-pinned in place.

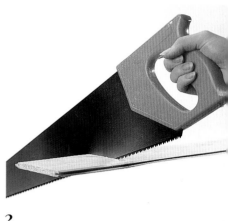

3

Makeshift trestles

Use two upturned chairs protected by cardboard and covered with a dust sheet to support your work if you do not have trestle tables.

4

5

6

7

8

9

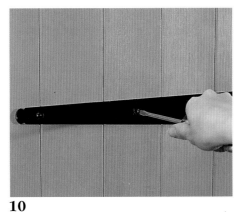

10

Step 6

When the glue has set completely, punch the nails slightly below the surface of the wood using a nail punch.

Day Two

Step 7

Fill the nail holes and any other imperfections in the finish with a sandable fine surface filler. Coat any knots in the wood with clear knotting solution. Apply and allow to dry according to the manufacturer's instructions. Re-hang the door.

Step 8

Sand any rough edges and the filled holes with sandpaper, starting with a coarse grade and finishing with a fine grade. Wipe away the sanding dust with a damp cloth. Give the door two coats of blue emulsion paint, leaving it to dry between coats.

Step 9

When the door is completely dry, paint with a coat of matt acrylic varnish.

Step 10

Hacksaw away the part of the strap hinge which fixes on to the door frame. Do the same to the other hinge, then fix both hinges to the door. Affix the handles and any other door furniture to finish.

Country kitchen makeover

It is hard to believe that this countrified kitchen, with its classic tongue-and-groove doors, started life as a distinctly un-rustic melamine flat pack.

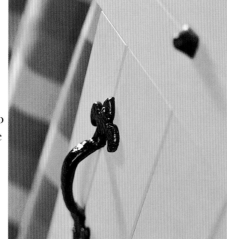

Flat pack melamine kitchen units are often the first choice for home owners on a budget. They are affordable, easy to clean, transport and assemble and as a result are enduringly popular. However, the overall effect created can be rather soulless, particularly if you are trying to create a lived-in country look. Handmade kitchens, which mimic the effect of a kitchen that has developed over the years from various antique pieces, are staggeringly expensive.

Here, then, is a simple way to add an exclusive, custom-made 'free standing' country kitchen feel to inexpensive chain store flat packs, which will be a godsend to all home decorators demoralised by mile upon mile of bumpy oatmeal melamine kitchen doors.

As with all the painted finishes described in this book, the success of the project depends largely on careful preparation. Time spent on scrupulous filling will unify the applied tongue-and-groove with the original melamine door so convincingly that even the most critical eye will not be able to detect that it is not a luxurious solid wood door.

The expanding, self-supporting curtain pole replaces the curtain wire and hook arrangement that you might expect to see on such a project. Chosen for its ease of use, since it requires no screwing into the cabinetry, it may be instantly retracted so the curtain can be washed. The pole also holds the curtain far more evenly than curtain wire, which tends to sag all too quickly. Choose a natural curtain fabric for an authentically homespun look.

Planning your time

DAY ONE
AM: Prepare doors. Blank out cabinetry with off-cuts of tongue-and-groove and skirting board

PM: Mark out tongue-and-groove. Cut to size and apply to doors. Fill. Paint doors and cabinetry

DAY TWO
AM: Varnish door. Re-hang when dry. Make curtain

PM: Hang curtain. Affix handle, hooks and studs

Tools and materials

Screwdriver

Sanding block and sandpaper

Tape measure and pencil

Lengths of tongue-and-groove board

Piece of skirting board

Panel saw

Wood adhesive

Panel pins

Nail punch

Hammer

Filler and filling knife

Emulsion paint

Paintbrush

Varnish and brush

Expanding, self-supporting curtain rod (often known as net rod)

Curtain fabric

Toning and tacking thread

Sewing machine

Pins, needles and fabric scissors

Iron

Insulating tape

Black metal door studs, hooks and handle

Screwdriver

Drill and 3mm ($\frac{1}{16}$ in) drill bit

Day One

Step 1

Remove the old handles. Sand the cupboards lightly to remove surface debris and wipe over with a damp cloth to remove resulting dust. This provides a good, smooth surface. Take the doors off the units.

Step 2

To blank out the top panel and uprights surrounding the door, cut lengths of tongue-and-groove boards to size and secure in place using wood adhesive and panel pins.

Step 3

To make the plinth, hold a length of skirting board in place, then work out what size piece of tongue-and-groove is needed to fill the resulting gap between the skirting board and the bottom of the cupboard. Cut the boards to size, then glue and panel pin in place, as shown in the step photograph.

Step 4

Work out how long the tongue-and-groove boards need to be by measuring the door panel. The panelling will look best if it slightly overhangs the existing door at the bottom edge.

Step 5

Working on the floor or a flat work surface, roughly assemble the tongue-and-groove boards and place the door on top to ascertain the width. The door will look neatest if the panels are centrally placed, so if the tongue-and-groove needs to be trimmed to fit, cut equal amounts from either side, rather than from one side only. Mark, then cut the tongue-and-groove to size.

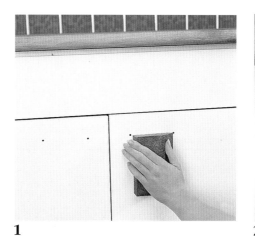

1

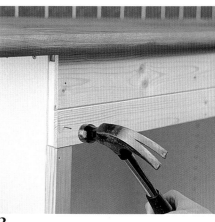

2

3

4

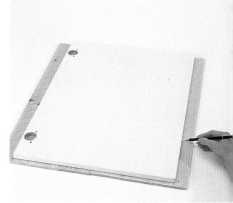

5

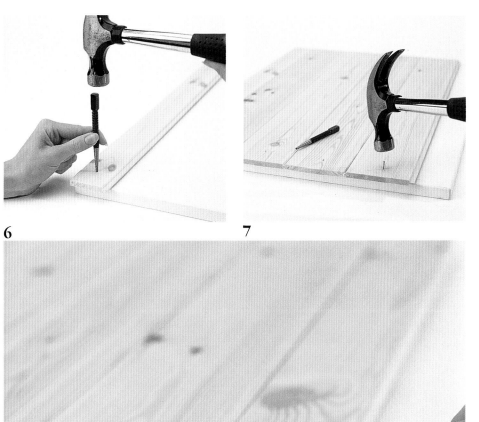

6

7

8

Step 6
Begin assembling the tongue-and-groove boards at the leading edge of the door, fixing the first piece in position with wood adhesive and panel pins. Tap the panel pins just below the surface of the wood, using a nail punch to ensure a neat finish.

Step 7
Continue to assemble the tongue-and-groove, glueing and pinning the pieces in this way. Tap the pieces together with a hammer to assemble firmly, using an offcut of wood to prevent damage to the tongue-and-groove itself.

Step 8
Fill any panel pin holes, as well as the line where the tongue-and-groove meets the door, with a fine surface filler. This will give a convincing, solid finish to both the door and to the cabinetry coverings.

Step 9
Paint the door, and the wood that has been applied to the cabinetry, using several coats of emulsion paint. Allow time for the paint to dry thoroughly between coats.

9

Paint magic
To achieve a slightly distressed look, brush on a diluted coat of emulsion paint in a slightly different colour to the main shade. Allow the colour beneath to show through.

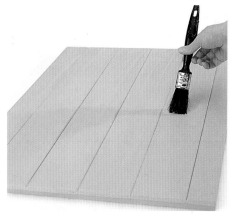

10

Day Two

Step 10

Varnish all paintwork, preferably using two or more coats of varnish. Allow the varnish to dry between coats.

Step 11

Re-hang the right-hand door and measure up for the curtain. The finished curtain will look best if it is the same length as the newly tongue-and-grooved door. Allowing for turnings, cut the fabric to approximately one and a half times the width of the actual gap.

Step 12

Fold under, press, tack and stitch the side and bottom hems of the curtain, allowing a sufficient casing at the top for smooth insertion of the curtain rod. Press to finish.

11

12

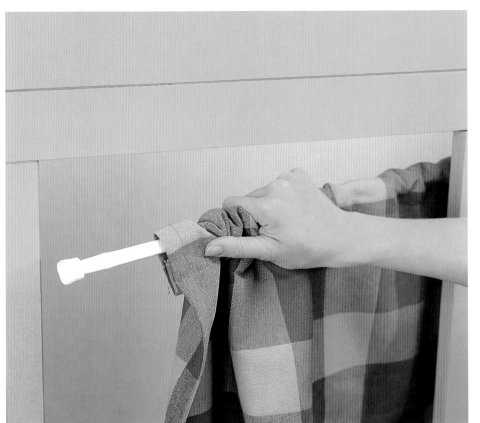

13

Step 13
Feed the curtain on to the expanding rod. Place the rod within the cupboard, behind the top panel, and expand the rod until it is the correct size to suspend itself. Wind a strip of insulating tape around the rod to prevent any movement of the curtain beyond the centre of the double unit.

Step 14
Drill pilot holes, then fix the new handle, tea towel hook and decorative studs in place on the door.

14

Smooth handling

New handles will transform any door. Choose handles to complement the decoration of the room, for example brushed aluminium for a sleek, contemporary look or heavy iron for traditional country charm.

Tool storage door

The back of a door is perfectly suited to storing the sort of fiddly-shaped and sized items that can cause storage nightmares, such as tools, sewing paraphernalia or gardening equipment.

An astonishing number of tools are acquired for basic DIY jobs such as wiring plugs and hanging pictures. This diverse array is most safely and usefully kept in some kind of organised format, where it may be easily viewed and swiftly accessed. Sharp blades are kept in one fixed place, not piled haphazardly into a tool box. For efficacy of use, the chisel and the screwdriver blades are prevented from blunting by being individually housed in a simple slotted shelf. If a tool can be swiftly located there is an increased chance that all those nagging DIY jobs will actually be attended to, instead of waiting for the moment when the screwdriver of a particular size is unearthed from wherever it was left after its last outing.

Hardware shops and DIY stores stock an enticing array of racking, pegboard, hooks and other items that can be used to turn a flat area into a hardworking tool store. Everyday objects can also be pressed into service. The nailing of jar lids into the underside of a shelf to provide clear storage for nails and screws has long been used in workshops and remains a brilliantly simple storage solution.

An increasing number of tools are being sold in inexpensive sets, complete with hanging racks, such as the screwdriver set shown here. Many tools are also being designed with storage in mind, for example some saws have a hole in the blade for hanging. Some items may not specifically be sold with hanging storage racks, but can be simply adapted. For example, boxed cases of small tools, such as drill bits, often have rigid plastic housings which grip the tools snugly. Simply screw the open case flat on to the door and you have a zero cost, minimal effort, perfectly sized storage area.

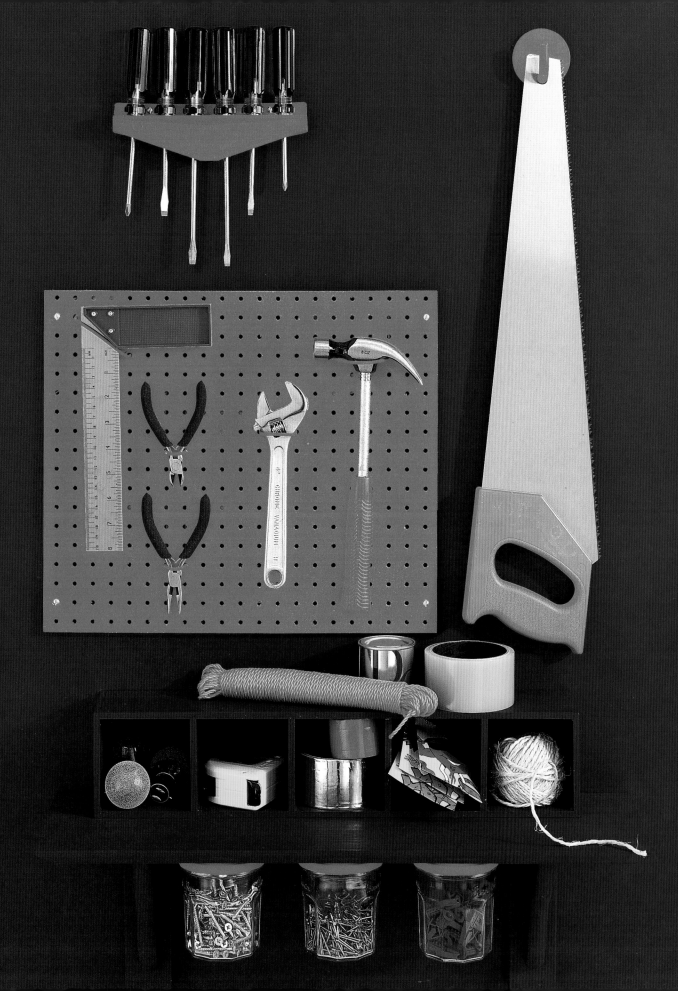

Day One

Step 1

Apply liquid sander to the door, following the manufacturer's directions. Paint, then varnish the door, leaving each coat to dry thoroughly before applying the next.

Step 2

Spray the door with primer, then spray paint the pegboard, wire, jar lids, saw hook and screwdriver store. Apply several thin coats of paint, rather than one thick coat, for a smooth, even result.

Step 3

Using cavity fixings, and following the manufacturer's directions, fix the screwdriver store to the door.

Step 4

Using cavity fixings, fix the hook for the saw to the door.

Step 5

Cut the pegboard to size. Fix the pegboard to the door with a flush door cavity fixing through one of the holes at each corner of the board. Pass the fixing through the pegboard first, then through two or three washers to stand the pegboard away from the door by slightly more than the thickness of the wire used in making the tool supports, and finally into the door.

Designing a tool store

Lay out all the tools you are likely to need to store before commencing the design of your tool store in order to get a clearer idea of what storage is needed; most people own many more tools than they imagine!

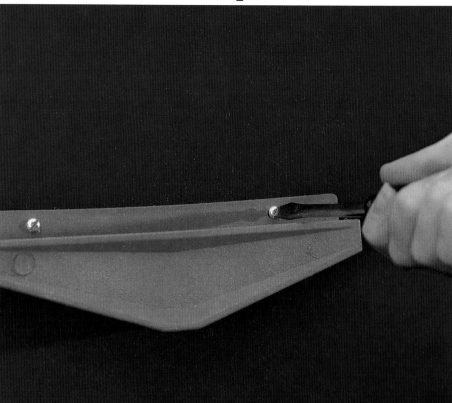

1

2

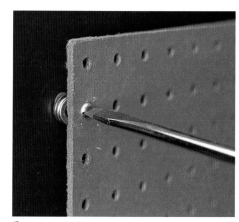

3

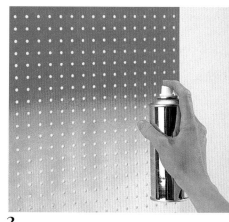

4

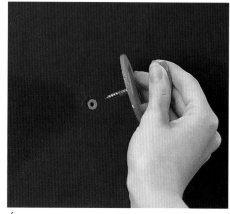

5

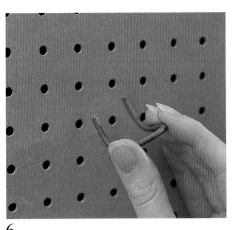

6

Alternative uses

If you want to store small items in the pigeonholes you could fix them to the shelf with the openings facing up. This will prevent items falling out when the door is opened.

Step 6

Bend stiff wire hoops to cradle your various tools. Bend each end of the wire into a right angle 'L' shape using pliers. Hold the wire securely in a vice for maximum ease of working. Pass the two 'L's' through two holes in the pegboard to secure the wire hooks in position.

Day Two

Step 7

Cut out the pigeon holes from a length of MDF (medium-density fibreboard). Assemble using a glue gun. Size the pigeon holes to suit your shelf and what you wish to store.

Step 8

Affix the shelf to the door using cavity fixings. Glue gun the pigeon holes to the shelf. Paint and varnish the pigeon holes and the shelf to match the door, allowing each coat to dry thoroughly before applying the next.

Step 9

Screw the jar lids on to the underside of the shelf, evenly spaced. Fill the jars with nails, screws and other items before introducing the jars to the lids.

7

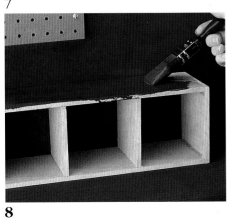

8

9

Wardrobe with fabric-lined doors

An inexpensive wardrobe takes on a cool Scandinavian elegance with this pretty fabric lining behind country-style wire fronted doors.

If you are purchasing a wardrobe specifically with this treatment in mind, look for one with panels that will be easy to remove. If such a piece is not available you will need to drill pilot holes just inside the existing panels at each corner, making a hole large enough to insert a jigsaw blade, then cut away the panels. More explicit instructions for cutting out a panel feature in the step-by-step instructions for making the Seashore bathroom cabinet on pages 24–9.

You may have an existing wardrobe that has no panels at all. There is a wide range of chain store and junk shop cabinetry available that is useful and inexpensive, yet featureless, which would respond admirably to this type of treatment, although producing a similar result on a flush door is inevitably more time-consuming than when working with a door with easily removable panels.

On a flush door, you will need to mark out the panels accurately before removing them with a jigsaw as described above. Depending on the structure of the door, you may be left with jagged, unattractive edges which will then need concealing with mitre-cut mouldings before embarking on the curtain making, painting and wire installation parts of the project. For the less than adventurous woodworker, finding a cupboard with removable panels will be key to the enjoyable and simple completion of this project.

Planning your time

DAY ONE
AM: Prepare doors. Mark screw holes for rods. Paint first coat

PM: Paint second coat. Spray paint chicken wire

DAY TWO
AM: Affix curtain brackets to doors. Secure chicken wire to doors

PM: Make and fit curtains. Attach new door knobs

Tools and materials

Screwdriver

Claw hammer

Tack lifter

Sanding block and sandpaper

Pencil

Tape measure

Metal ruler

Drill

3mm (1/16 in) drill bit

Masking tape

Blue paint

Paintbrush

Chicken wire

Zinc, grey and white spray primer

Old blanket

Thick gloves

Wire cutters

Rod brackets and screws

Staple gun and staples

Curtain rod

Tube cutter

Fabric

Toning and tacking thread

Iron

Pins and needle

Fabric scissors

Replacement door knobs

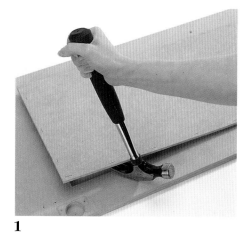

1

Day One

Step 1

Remove the doors from the wardrobe and take off the old handles. Lever out the door panels using a claw hammer.

Step 2

Remove any protruding staples or nails with a tack lifter, or make them safe by bending them over. Sand the edges of the panels smooth.

Step 3

Mark the position of the screws which will hold the curtain rod bracket with a pencilled cross. The rod will need to be placed sufficiently high so that the stitch line of the curtain casing will not be visible from the front of the door.

2

3

6

Step 4

Drill the pilot holes and lightly
sand them smooth. A useful way of
indicating the correct drilling depth is
to mark the 3mm (⅛ in) drill bit with
tape, marking a depth which should be
nearly equal to the length of the screw.

Step 5

Paint the wardrobe and doors inside
and out with two coats of blue paint,
allowing the paint to dry thoroughly
between coats.

Step 6

Working in a well-ventilated area, with
all surfaces protected against over
spray, lightly spray the chicken wire
with grey and white primer to age.

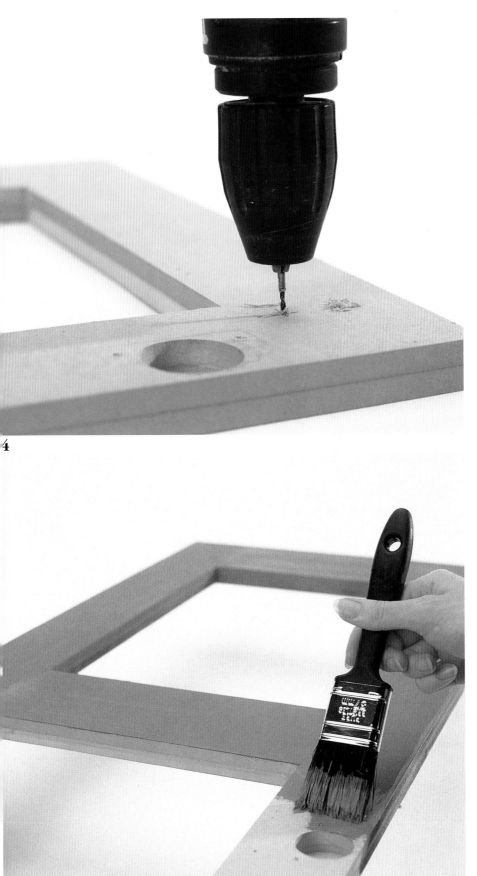

4

5

Day Two

Step 7

Place something soft, such as an old blanket, on the work surface to protect the new paintwork. Place the doors face down on this soft surface. Spread chicken wire across the openings then, wearing thick gloves, cut the chicken wire to size using wire cutters.

Step 8

Screw the brackets for the curtain rods in place, as marked in steps 3 and 4, at the top of each door.

Step 9

Staple the chicken wire in place on the back of the doors.

Step 10

Carefully, trim any remaining raw edges of the chicken wire with the wire cutters. You may wish to wear gloves to protect your hands.

Step 11

Measure and cut the curtain rod to length using a tube cutter. The rod will need to be slightly shorter than the distance between the brackets. Any shortfall in length will be absorbed when the collars are fitted.

7

8

9

10

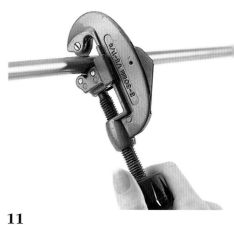

11

14

12

13

Step 12

Temporarily install the curtain rods, fitting the collar to one bracket and inserting the rod. Slide the remaining collar over the other end of the rod. Secure the collars loosely.

Step 13

Measure the distance between the outside edges of the curtain rods to ascertain curtain sizes. Add an extra 50mm (2in) at each end for a double turning. Cut off fabric selvedges. Allow twice as much fabric as the actual width of each opening, plus turnings, for a good degree of fullness. Double turn and make a narrow hem along the side seams, then press. Double turn the fabric to make generous casings at each end of the curtain; pin, tack and stitch. Press.

Step 14

Remove one end of each curtain collar. Slide on the curtain, right side facing the chicken wire. Tighten the collar to secure. Replace doors on wardrobe and add the new door knobs.

Adding privacy to a half-glazed door

A simple fabric panel adds discretion and style to what was a less than lovely half-glazed door.

Planning your time

DAY ONE
AM: Rub down paintwork

PM: Paint door

DAY TWO
AM: Varnish paintwork

PM: Cut voile and staple in place.
Trim and apply braid. Replace handle

Tools and materials

Screwdriver

Liquid sander and cloth

Rags

Emulsion paint
(coloured to suit voile)

Paintbrush and paint kettle

Stirring stick

Varnish and varnish brush

Scissors

Piece of voile
(to suit door panel)

Iron

Tape measure

Straight edge

Black marker

Staple gun

Staples

Gimp/braid

Glue gun and glue sticks

Many homes have a door like this, perfectly sound and functional, yet unattractive. The glazed area allows light in but the glass is often unspeakably ugly or may even be clear, allowing no privacy at all. This simple solution allows light to pass uninterrupted into your home, but softens the patterning of the occluded glass, or masks the clarity of an unwanted expanse of plain glass. The voile looks equally pretty from the other side of the door.

There is an increasingly wide range of patterned voiles on the market; some embroidered or printed with colours as well as the self-patterned example used here. Painting the door in the dominant colour of a patterned voile would be very pretty. The ethereal cream on cream scheme chosen here was a definite reaction against the original heavy brown gloss which formerly dressed the door.

Choose the braid trim to suit the mood of the room. Here, we wanted to produce a subtle, classy result and used a calm, toning braid. If your colour scheme is more vibrant, you can be bolder. You may choose a plain, richly coloured voile, for example in midnight blue or burnt orange and partner it with a dramatically contrasting braid, then trim with oversized decorative nails. Whatever you decide, changing the voile when you change your scheme is simplicity itself. Rip off the braid and fabric, pull out the staples with a screwdriver or staple remover, and start again. If you need to return the door to its original state, fill the staple holes, repaint, and replace the original handle.

Adding new door furniture instantly changes the mood of the door. Specialist ironmongers produce enticing mail order catalogues, and are well worth searching out when you are re-dressing your doors.

Day One

Step 1

Remove the old door handle. Apply liquid sander to the door, following the manufacturer's directions.

Step 2

Paint the entire door with emulsion and leave to dry. Apply further coats of paint if necessary for a good opaque coverage, allowing each coat to dry thoroughly before applying the next.

Day Two

Step 3

Varnish the paintwork and leave to dry. For added durability add further coats of varnish, allowing each coat to dry thoroughly before applying the next.

Step 4

Cut a piece of voile approximately 15cm (6in) larger on each side than the glazed area. It is necessary to allow the extra voile so that you will have something to pull on whilst stretching the fabric to fit. Most of the excess will be trimmed off later. Iron the voile.

Step 5

Draw a line in black marker 20mm (¾in) around the glass area on the door. This will be the staple line and will be covered by decorative braid later.

Removing staples

Inaccurately placed staples can be removed by pushing a thin bladed screwdriver under the bridge of the staple and levering gently upwards. Grip the exposed staple with pliers if necessary to remove completely.

1

2

3

4

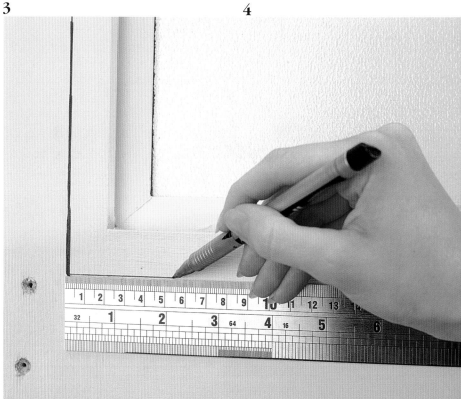

5

6

Working with voile

Make sure that the grain of the fabric remains perpendicular to ensure a smart, smooth result. It is easy to distort such a fragile fabric with process of pulling it taut and stapling it to the door, the unsightly results of which may not be noticed until the voile is in place.

7

8

Step 6

Position the voile centrally over the glass area and put one staple through the voile into the woodwork in the middle of the top black line. Stretch the voile slightly towards the ends of the line and place another staple at each end. Fill the top line with staples.

Step 7

Stretch the voile slightly towards the middle of the bottom line under the glass panel and staple. Continue stapling to each side of the central staple, pulling gently to even out any stretch marks as work progresses. Stretch the voile equally between the left and the right marker lines and staple similarly so that all uneven tension in the fabric is removed and the voile is evenly taut and smooth.

Step 8

Trim all the edges of the voile to within 4mm (⅛in) of the stapled line, using a pair of sharp scissors.

Step 9

Apply a length of gimp or braid to cover the staple line and the raw edge of the fabric, using a glue gun to secure it in position. Fold the braid to make neatly mitred corners. Add the new handle to the door.

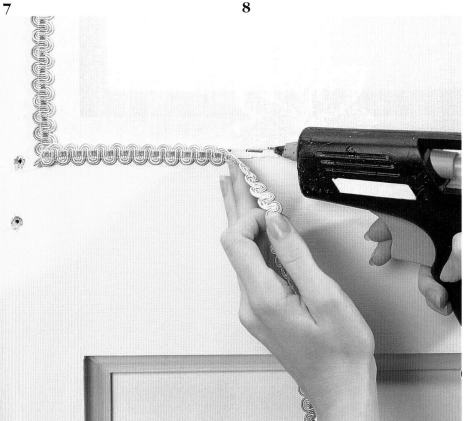

9

Securing the voile

If you do not want to invest in a staple gun, simply use upholstery nails or gimp pins (available from most hardware stores) to secure the voile. Tap in with a hammer. Decorative upholstery nails could also be used to trim the braid border.

Child's fantasy wardrobe

Children need every possible incentive to put away their toys and clothes. This fun cupboard may just lead to a tidier room.

Junk shops are a good source of very inexpensive, serviceable, but challengingly awful looking wardrobes. Even what at first glance might appear to be a truly unappealing wardrobe or cupboard can be simply transformed into a real scene stealer with a little imagination and lateral thinking.

The window-like framework on the doors of this chain-store buy suggested this simple, yet effective, design which incorporates a number of different colours and textures for visual and tactile interest. If your wardrobe has flat doors and you wish to replicate the window design illustrated here it would be relatively easy to glue a 'window frame' of mounting board or wood in place.

This type of fantasy project benefits from an open and relaxed approach to its design. If the exact flowers, fabrics and frame shown here cannot be found, do not worry. This design metamorphosed as it was produced and as quite different materials from those originally envisaged came to hand. Have fun gathering material for this project with the child who will eventually own the wardrobe. They will lead you in the direction of some of the most unlikely, yet imaginative objects, such as the ugly floral candle rings which yielded the adorable painted wooden ladybirds and the shoelaces decorated with bright wooden beads which form the tiebacks.

Planning your time

DAY ONE
AM: Prepare and paint first coat on wardrobe, mounting board and doors

PM: Paint second coat. Make and affix sky panels. Make curtains

DAY TWO
AM: Assemble pelmets. Attach tieback hooks and arrange tiebacks

PM: Attach handles and decorations

Tools and materials

Sanding block and sandpaper

Paintbrush

Lime green paint

Mounting board

Thin card

Pencil

Metal ruler

Scissors

Blue cotton fabric

Multi-purpose spray adhesive

Vividly striped cotton fabric

Needle and thread

19 x 19mm (¾ x ¾ in) softwood

Handsaw

Drill and 4mm (⅛ in) drill bit

1¼in No.8 woodscrews x 4

Screwdriver

Staple gun and staples

Cutting mat

Craft knife and blades

Glue gun and glue sticks

Handles

Shoelaces and wooden beads

Tieback hooks

Bradawl

Plywood flowers and decorations

Inflatable sun mirror frame

Double-sided adhesive tape

Day One

Step 1

Lightly rub down the wardrobe to
remove any surface debris and provide
a key for the paint. Wipe over with a
damp cloth to remove sanding dust.

Step 2

Paint the wardrobe, doors and
mounting board with two coats of lime
green paint, allowing each coat to dry
thoroughly before applying the next.
There is no need to paint the recessed
panels as these will be covered when
the wardrobe is complete.

1

2

Subtle style

If painting and decorating the
wardrobe to suit an older child, or
even a teenager, use muted neutral
shades of paint and match with
natural fabrics.

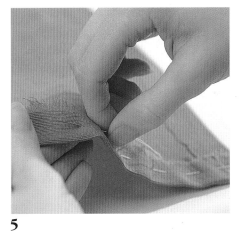

5

3

4

Step 3

Mark out and cut panels of thin card to fit within the door panels, allowing room for the fabric to be wrapped around the card. Cut the piece of electric blue fabric to size, allowing sufficient extra to wrap around the card. Spray one side of the card and the reverse of the fabric with adhesive. Glue the fabric on to the card, turning excess fabric to the reverse, and snipping at the corners to produce a neat, mitred finish with no bulk.

Step 4

Glue the fabric-covered pieces of card in place within each of the recessed door panels with spray adhesive.

Step 5

Cut pieces of striped fabric to form the curtains, allowing a small excess for turnings. Hem the sides and bottom edge of the curtains by spraying the edges of the fabric with adhesive and turning a seam allowance to the underside of the fabric. Run a gathering stitch along the top of each curtain, and draw up to the desired fullness.

Day Two

Step 6

Cut a length of 19 x 19mm (¾ x ¾ in) softwood to fit neatly along the centre top of each door panel. Mark the position of the screw holes with a pencil, 50mm (2in) in from each end of this batten. Drill through at these marks with a 5mm (¼in) drill bit. Screw the battens in place.

Step 7

Using the staple gun, staple the curtains on to the battens and beyond the battens on to the door surround to cover the width of each door.

Step 8

Cut a length of painted mounting board to sit on, and extend beyond the batten. Make sure it is sufficient to allow for the fullness of the curtains. This will support the front face of the pelmet. Cut two small lengths of card to support each end of this piece. Staple these three pieces on to the top and ends of each batten.

Step 9

Cut lengths of painted mounting board to form the decorative fascia of each pelmet. On the reverse side, draw a line 25mm (1in) in from one of the long edges. Mark along this line and along the edge of each board at 20mm (¾in) intervals. Join up the alternate marks to produce a zigzag design.

Step 10

On a cutting mat, cut out the zigzag pattern with a craft knife and metal rule. Paint the raw edges and leave to dry. Assemble the pelmets on the wardrobe, using a glue gun.

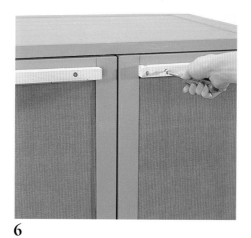

6

7

8

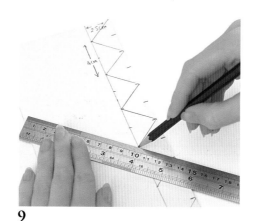

9

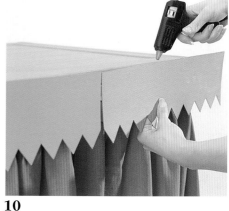

10

11

12

Step 11
Screw the new handles in place on each door.

Step 12
Thread wooden beads on to brightly coloured shoe laces and knot the ends. Place around curtain to work out their desired length and placement. Mark the position of the tie-back hooks on the wardrobe. Make a pilot hole with a bradawl, then screw in the hooks and arrange the tie-backs.

Step 13
Glue buttons and pompoms on to the centres of plywood flowers. Glue the flowers in position on the cupboard using a glue gun, then secure the ladybirds in place on the flowers.

Step 14
Affix the inflatable sun mirror frame to the right hand door with double-sided adhesive tape.

13

Fantastic voyage

Customize the wardrobe for a boy by painting it with rugged camouflage colours. Decorate the painted wardrobe with a variety of exciting textures, from thin metal sheeting to sandpaper and rubber car mats.

14

Glossary

Artists' brushes

Countersink bit

Epoxy putty

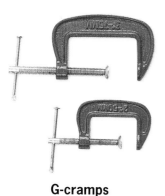

G-cramps

Acrylic eggshell paint
Fast-drying, but tough paint with a satin sheen that is often used as a base coat. Solvent-based eggshell paint is also available, although it does take much longer to dry.

Acrylic artists' paints
Artists' acrylic paints are available in a variety of colours from art shops. Supplied in tubes and pots.

Acrylic varnish
A water-based varnish available in spray or liquid form. Has an opaque finish when applied but dries clear. Quick drying, it will not yellow with age, unlike oil-based varnish.

Artists' brushes
Available in different sizes, artists' brushes are ideal for painting details. Often made from squirrel hair, the bristles do not separate.

Bradawl
A tool used to mark a small hole in wood before fixing panel pins or screws – the starter hole helps prevent the wood from splitting.

Cotton buds
Indispensable for cleaning fiddly areas or removing paint splashes; also for applying knotting fluid.

Countersink bit
An attachment for a drill that enlarges the top part of a previously drilled hole to allow the screw head to sit just below the level of the wood.

Crackle glaze
Water-based glaze applied between two coats of matt emulsion paint, that produces cracks between the two when the top coat dries.

Découpage
This is an old Victorian technique which literally means to 'cut out', and involves decorating a surface using cut-out paper images. The Victorians built up the finished surface with several coats of varnish, until there was no variation in the surface texture, in order to create a hand-painted look.

Drill/drill bits
When buying a power drill make sure that the motor is powerful enough for all tasks; some drills with very low speed settings can also be used for putting in screws. Bits are available in different sizes for drilling different-sized holes.

Emulsion paint
Matt emulsion paint is a versatile water-based paint that can be used on most surfaces. It is quick drying and is available in a wide range of colours.

Epoxy putty
A two-part putty that is used to repair broken plumbing. The parts begin to harden as soon as they are mixed, giving about 20 minutes working time. The putty has a pliable, uniform consistency that can be filed and sanded to an even greater smoothness when dry.

G-cramps
Invaluable alternative to an extra pair of hands. These simple devices are available in several sizes, and grip two or more pieces of wood together while you work.

Hacksaw
A small saw for cutting metal.

Jigsaw
An power saw that allows you to cut intricate shapes. It has a base plate that can be angled for cutting. Different grades of blade give a different quality of cut.

Knotting fluid
Solution applied to seal knots in wood and to prevent resin seeping through. Not necessary for old wood that has fully dried out or for new wood that has been kiln dried.

Masking tape
Useful for masking a surface adjacent to an area being painted.

Medium-density fibreboard (MDF)
Smooth, dense board made from compressed wood fibres. Ask for the formaldehyde-free type.

Mitre saw
Saw with selectable fixed angles and support to cut mitred joints accurately and simply.

Panel pins
Small steel or copper nails without a head, which means that they lie flush with the level of wood so that the tops are not visible.

Plywood
Thin veneers of wood bonded together in alternating layers so that the grain goes in different directions, giving strength and pliability. Usually made with wood with an attractive grain.

Sandpaper/sanding block
Sheets of sandpaper, or abrasive paper, are available in various grades, from fine, for finishing work, to coarse grade or grit for heavier work. For ease of use, sandpaper can be wrapped around a cork block, known as a sanding block.

Staple gun
Larger than a domestic stapler, a staple gun is very powerful and can be used to secure a piece of fabric on to wood.

Varnishing brush
A flat brush specifically designed for varnishing but useful for all paintwork. Varnishing brushes hold a large amount of varnish or paint and have very fine bristles.

Wax
Usually used as a final coat, but can be used as a finish on its own.

Wood filler
Ideal for filling holes, buy ready-to-use filler in a tube or tub. Apply with a filler knife. When dry, the filler can be sanded smooth.

Mitre saw

Staple gun

Sanding block

Varnishing brush

Suppliers

The author and publishers would like to thank the following suppliers:

Clayton Munroe Ltd
Kingston West Drive
Kingston
Staverton
Totnes
Devon
TQ9 6AR
Tel. 01803 762626

Handle for Transforming a plain, flush door project, page 38.

Forbo Nairn
Brochure hotline tel. 0345 023 166

Linoleum flooring in Child's fantasy wardrobe project, page 68.

Pilkingtons Tiles
P.O. Box 4
Clifton Junction
Manchester
M27 8LP
Tel. 0161 727 1001

Terracotta tiles in Citrus kitchen cupboard project, page 12.

Swish Products
Available from DIY stores and soft furnishing suppliers nationwide. Call for details of stockists.
Tel. 0121 236 9501

Self supporting, expanding curtain rod (medium weight net rod) for Country kitchen makeover project, page 48.

Templates

Floral finger plate and doorknob set

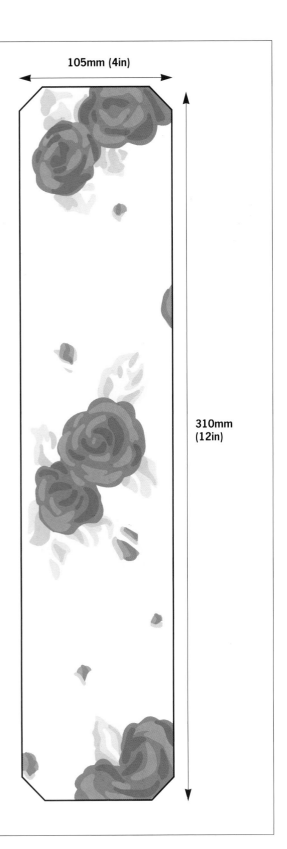

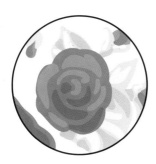

These templates are intended as rough, positional guides only. Build up the floral design using relaxed, swirling brush strokes. Start by applying a pale tone of paint and build up with darker tones. Practise first on a offcut of MDF.

105mm (4in)

310mm (12in)

Templates

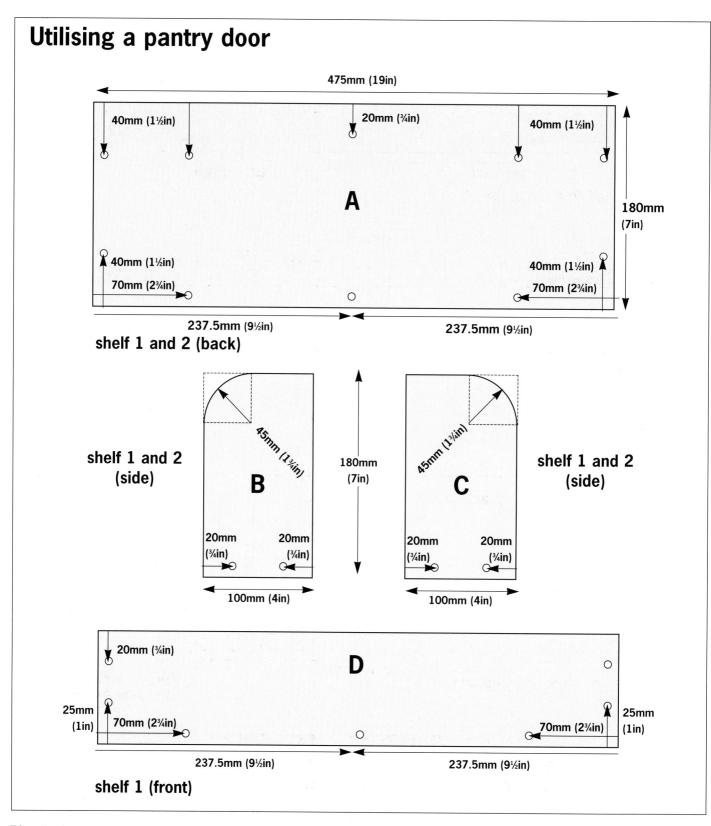

Utilising a pantry door

A

475mm (19in)

40mm (1½in) 20mm (¾in) 40mm (1½in)

180mm (7in)

40mm (1½in) 40mm (1½in)

70mm (2¾in) 70mm (2¾in)

237.5mm (9½in) 237.5mm (9½in)

shelf 1 and 2 (back)

B

shelf 1 and 2 (side)

45mm (1¾in)

180mm (7in)

20mm (¾in) 20mm (¾in)

100mm (4in)

C

shelf 1 and 2 (side)

45mm (1¾in)

20mm (¾in) 20mm (¾in)

100mm (4in)

D

20mm (¾in)

25mm (1in) 25mm (1in)

70mm (2¾in) 70mm (2¾in)

237.5mm (9½in) 237.5mm (9½in)

shelf 1 (front)

Templates

Utilising a pantry door

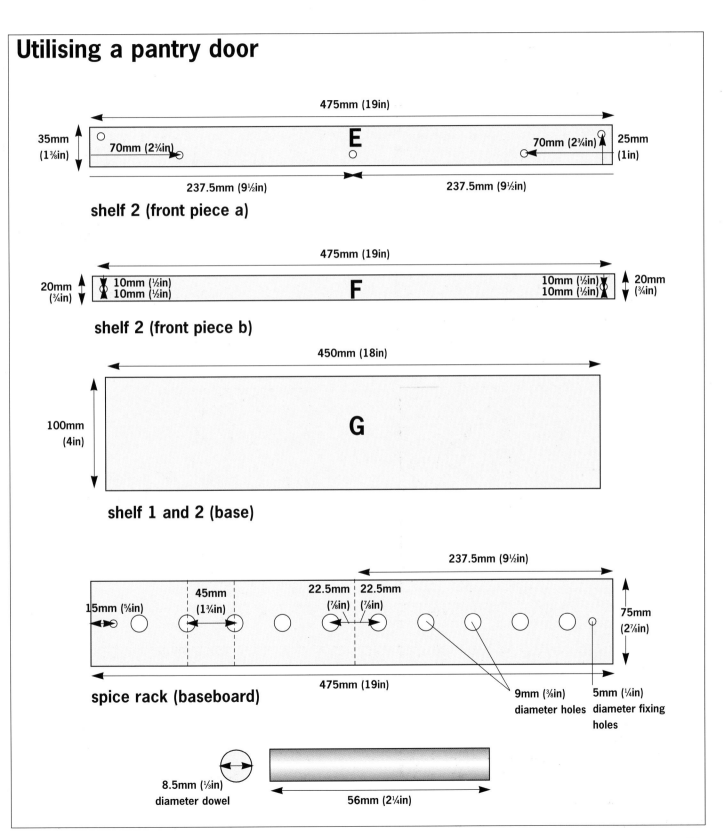

475mm (19in)

35mm (1⅜in)

70mm (2¾in)

E

70mm (2¾in)

25mm (1in)

237.5mm (9½in)

237.5mm (9½in)

shelf 2 (front piece a)

475mm (19in)

20mm (¾in)

10mm (½in)
10mm (½in)

F

10mm (½in)
10mm (½in)

20mm (¾in)

shelf 2 (front piece b)

450mm (18in)

100mm (4in)

G

shelf 1 and 2 (base)

237.5mm (9½in)

15mm (⅝in)

45mm (1¾in)

22.5mm (⅞in) 22.5mm (⅞in)

75mm (2⅞in)

475mm (19in)

spice rack (baseboard)

9mm (⅜in) diameter holes

5mm (¼in) diameter fixing holes

8.5mm (⅓in) diameter dowel

56mm (2¼in)

Index

B
bathroom cabinet, seashore, 24-9
blocking-in, 8
bottle shelves, 18–23

C
calligraphy, 16, 38, 42-3
cavity fixings, 18
child's fantasy wardrobe, 68-73
coloured wood dyes, 30, 31, 33
cottage-style door, 44-7
countersink bit, 74
crackle glaze, 24, 74
cupboards:
    citrus kitchen cupboard, 12-17
    romantic cupboard, 34-7
    seashore bathroom cabinet, 24-9
curtain poles/rods, 48, 52-3, 62-3
curtains:
    child's fantasy wardrobe, 71-2
    country kitchen makeover, 48, 52-3
    wardrobe with fabric-lined doors, 63

D
découpage, 74
    citrus kitchen cupboard, 12, 17
    transforming a plain, flush door, 42
distressed paint effect, 51
door knob and finger plate set, 8-11
doors:
    adding privacy to a half-glazed door,
      64-7
    child's fantasy wardrobe, 68-73
    cottage-style door, 44-7
    stripping and finishing a pine door,
      30-3
    transforming a plain, flush, door, 38-43
    tool storage door, 54-7
    utilizing a pantry door, 18-23
    wardrobe with fabric-lined doors, 58-63
drill depths, 22
dyes, coloured wood, 30, 31, 33

E
epoxy putty, 34, 37, 74

F
fabric:
    child's fantasy wardrobe, 68, 71-2
    country kitchen makeover, 48, 52-3
    romantic cupboard, 34-7
    wardrobe with fabric-lined doors,
      58-63
finger plate and door knob set, 8-11
floral designs:
    child's fantasy wardrobe, 68-73
    finger plate and door knob set, 8-11
    romantic cupboard, 34-7
    transforming a plain, flush door, 42-3

H
half-glazed door, adding privacy to, 64-7
handles:
    choosing, 6, 53
    citrus kitchen cupboard, 17
    seashore bathroom cabinet, 29
    see also knobs
hinges, strap, 44, 47

K
kitchen cupboard, citrus, 12-17
kitchen makeover, country, 48-53
knobs:
    finger plate and door knob set, 8-11
    romantic cupboard, 34, 37
    see also handles
knotting, 75

L
larder *see* pantry
liquid sanders, 24, 38

M
melamine units:
    citrus kitchen cupboard, 12-17
    country kitchen makeover, 48-53
mitre saw, 14, 15, 75
modelling medium, 34, 37
mouldings:
    citrus kitchen cupboard, 12-16
    transforming a plain, flush door, 38-43

P
paint effects:
    distressed, 51
    Swedish style finish, 30, 31, 33
paints, 7, 18, 74
paint stripping, 30, 32
pantry doors, utilizing, 18-23
pine doors, stripping and finishing, 30-3
projecting text, 22, 23
putty, epoxy, 34, 37, 74

S
sander, liquid, 24, 38
seashore bathroom cabinet, 24-9
shadowbox frame, 24-9
spice racks, 18-23
staples, removing, 66
stencils, kitchen cupboard, 16
strap hinges, 44, 47
Swedish style finish, 30, 31, 33

T
text, painting, 16, 38, 42-3
tongue-and-groove boards:
    cottage-style door, 44-7
    country kitchen makeover, 48-53
tool storage door, 54-7
trestles, makeshift, 46

U
universal stainers, 75

V
varnish, 30, 31, 33, 74
Victorian finish, 30, 31, 33
voile half-glazed door, 64-7

W
wardrobes:
    child's fantasy wardrobe, 68-73
    wardrobe with fabric-lined doors, 58-63
wax finishes, 30, 31, 33
window design, child's fantasy wardrobe,
    68-73
wood dyes, 30, 31, 33